# Becky's Braids

written by Susan Weiss
illustrated by Deborah Gross-Zuchman

ABINGDON SQUARE PUBLISHING
New York

Copyright © 2017 Susan Weiss and Deborah Gross-Zuchman

All rights reserved.
No part of this publication may be reproduced in any manner, stored in a retrieval system, or transmitted in any form by any means—electronic, mechanical, photocopying, recording or otherwise—without written permission from the publisher, except in article reviews.

**BECKY'S BRAIDS**
is published by
Abingdon Square Publishing Ltd.
463 West Street, Suite G122
New York, NY 10014 USA
www.abingdonsquarepublishing.com

Text © 2017 by Susan Weiss
Artwork © 2017 by Deborah Gross-Zuchman

ISBN 978-0-692-89939-7
Library of Congress Control Number: 2017961809
First Edition
Printed in the United States of America

---

Dedicated to all the Grandmothers who share their love, wisdom and patience.
Thanks to all the little girls with messy hair who inspired this story.

Loving thanks to our husbands, Ken Weiss and Philip Zuchman who encouraged these two grandmothers in writing and illustrating this book.

"If nothing is going well, call your grandmother." – Italian Proverb

Becky had the messiest hair.
She did not like it washed.
She did not like it combed.
She did not like it brushed.
She did not like barrettes.
She did not like headbands.
She did not like rubber bands.

In the morning, Becky's mother would try to brush her hair.
Becky would shout, "NO!"
In the tub, when her mom would wash her hair, Becky would squirm, wiggle and make a fuss.

One day, Becky's grandma
came to visit - for a whole week.
Becky loved Grandma's visits.
There was always something special
to do each day.

Monday, they went to the library. But, before they left the house, Becky's Mom asked if she could fix her hair.
"NO WAY!" shouted Becky.

Becky took home a giant pile of books from the library. Grandma read every one. Becky held her hair back from her eyes so she could see the pictures.

Up with the sun on Tuesday,
Becky's hair was a mess but off she went with
Grandma to feed the ducks.
She came back with duck feathers in her
tangled, messy hair.

Wednesday came and Becky's hair
was a disaster!
She didn't care and went for ice cream
with Grandma.
Her hair fell into her ice cream. Yuk!

Thursday, they planted flowers.
Bits of flowers and potting soil dusted her hair.

Friday came and Becky didn't know what Grandma had planned.

"I think you're old enough to help me make challah for tonight's Sabbath dinner. Would you like to help?"
"Yes!" Becky shouted excitedly.

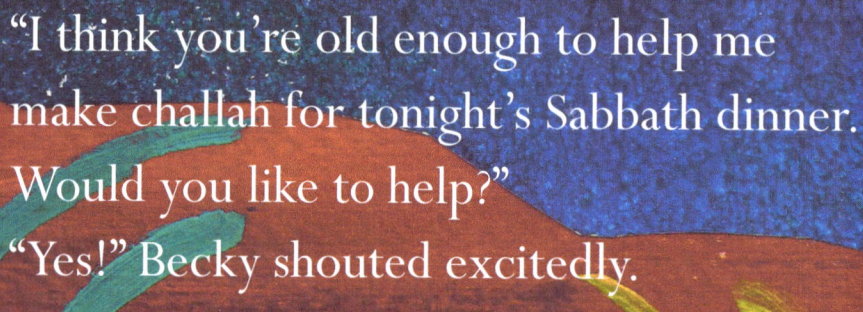

Together they sifted the flour and beat the eggs. They mixed the yeast and oil and kneaded the dough. Then they placed the mixture into a bowl.

Grandma told Becky, "To make sure the challah dough grows, you have to treat it like a new baby. It needs to be handled gently and kept clean, covered and warm."

Becky carefully took the bowl of dough, covered it with a dish towel and put it in a warm place in the kitchen.

One hour later Becky peeked under the cover.
WOW!
The dough had grown twice as big.

Grandma divided the dough into six parts.
They rolled out six long ropes of dough.
Using the first three ropes, Grandma showed
Becky how to braid the challah.
Over, under, over, under, until they got to the end.
Then they did the same with the second three ropes.
Again, they covered the dough to rest and grow.

One hour passed, the dough had grown and they painted the loaves with egg and honey to make them sweet and shiny.
Into the oven the challahs went.
OHHHHH, the kitchen smelled so good!

Twenty minutes later, the challahs were ready.
They were golden brown and beautiful.
Becky told her Grandma they were the most beautiful things ever.

"You know, Becky," Grandma replied,
"I can make your hair look like two beautiful challahs."
"No, you can't," laughed Becky.
"I can. Ask your mother for shampoo, a towel,
a brush, a comb and two barrettes."

Becky was so excited she forgot to say no and
ran to her mother.
Becky told her, "Grandma is going to make challah
on my head."
"I've got to see this," said her mother.

Grandma said, "First, we have to gather our ingredients. I need clean, shiny hair."

"You can wash my hair in the tub, Grandma," said Becky. Into the tub jumped Becky and Grandma washed, dried and brushed Becky's hair. "What's next?" shouted Becky.

"I need two barrettes," said Grandma. Becky ran off and collected the two barrettes and gave them to Grandma. "Next, we will separate your hair into six parts, just like the dough. Three on this side of your face and three on the other. Next, I will braid these ropes just like the challahs. When I get to the end I will clip them shut with the barrettes.

Grandma finished and Becky looked into the mirror.

There, on either side of her face, were two beautiful, neat braids just like the gorgeous challahs she and Grandma made.

"Mom," shouted Becky, "can you make challahs on my head every day?"
"Certainly," she smiled at her daughter and winked at her mother.
Becky never yelled when her hair was washed, brushed and braided …
… and never had messy hair again.

Becky had challah braids that she wore proudly.

# Becky's Challah

Ingredients (makes three medium or two large loaves)

### Dough
1 tbsp. active dry yeast
½ cup sugar
2 cups warm water (110° F)
9 cups of white bread flour
(or 3 cups of whole wheat and 6 cups of white bread flour)
4 large eggs at room temperature
½ cup vegetable oil
1 tbsp. salt
½ cup sugar
Small bowl of warm water (to keep hands wet and help incorporate mixture of flour)

### Glaze
1 egg
2 tsp sugar or honey

### Directions
1. Mix the yeast and 1/3 cup sugar in warm water, stir to dissolve and let the mixture stand until a foam forms on the top (approx ten minutes). Mix in 3 cups of the flour.
2. Beat the 4 eggs with vegetable oil, salt and 1/2 cup of sugar. Add this mixture to the yeast mixture. Combine well. Continue to add and mix remaining 6 cups of flour 1 cup at a time. Using hands, continue to mix dipping hands into warm water if needed to incorporate all the flour. Turn the dough out onto a floured surface and gently knead for 5 minutes.
3. Form the dough into a large ball and place in a greased bowl. Turn the ball once to cover with oil.
4. Cover and place in a warm location. Leave until it is double in size (about one hour)
5. Turn dough out onto floured surface. Cut into thirds for 3 loaves or in half for 2 loaves.
6. Cut each third or half into thirds. Roll each third into ropes approximately 14 inches long. Braid the 3 ropes starting in the middle to end then repeat on other side. Pinch and tuck under the end of each braided side.
7. Place loaves on parchment paper lined cookie sheets. Cover and let rise 45 minutes.
8. Mix glaze and lightly brush loaves. Sprinkle loaves with poppy or sesame seeds.
9. Bake in preheated 350° F oven for 25 minutes. Cool loaves on cooling rack.

Susan Weiss is a retired psychiatric nurse and psychopharmacology researcher. Although published in her professional field, this is her first published children's book. Susan is an accomplished home chef and loves to bake Challah with her twin granddaughters, Ever and Simone.
They were the inspiration for this story.

Deborah Gross-Zuchman, a Philadelphia painter, was an art teacher in the Philadelphia public schools. She also worked as a project manager for the Philadelphia Mural Arts Program. Gross-Zuchman uses the technique of collage as painting with paper, cutting up her hand painted papers creating interesting and surprising effects.

    A book of her poems and paintings, *Windows Into War (A Mother's Lament)* is published by Abingdon Square Publishers, NY. *Seder for the 21st Century, a Passover Haggadah,* has an emphasis on social justice and freedom and is illustrated with her collages.
www.deborahzuchman.com

www.ingramcontent.com/pod-product-compliance
Lightning Source LLC
Chambersburg PA
CBHW060808090426
42736CB00002B/204